How Much Water Do We Have?

"As a husband, father, friend, and business professional, I found many ways that the 'five waters' discussed in Pete Nunweiler's book will help me become even better in each aspect of my life. 'How much water do we have?' is a question I'll often ask myself day-in, day-out."

—*JR Espino, national field training manager*

"Clear, concise, and to the point."

—*Cooper Krajewski, RN, CCRN*

"Insightful and inspiring, *How Much Water Do We Have?* leaves you ready to embrace the next challenge—personally and professionally."

—*Heather Chester, non-profit development and event manager*

"I love that *How Much Water Do We Have?* is a workbook with questions and that real life stories are weaved throughout. I didn't want to put it down! The stories make it come to life and show the choice that we all have every day to challenge our own thinking to determine our outcome."

—*Karla Verdi, senior field training manager*

How Much Water Do We Have?

5 Success Principles for
Conquering Any Challenge and
Thriving in Times of Change

Pete Nunweiler with Kris Nunweiler

How Much Water Do We Have?
© 2016 by Pete Nunweiler

This book is available at special discounts when purchased in quantity for use as premiums, promotions, fundraising, and educational use. For details, contact: shelley@daveburgessconsulting.com.

Published by Dave Burgess Consulting, Inc.
San Diego, CA
http://daveburgessconsulting.com

Cover Design by Genesis Kohler
Editing and Interior Design by My Writers' Connection

Library of Congress Control Number: 2016931723
Paperback ISBN: 978-0-9861555-6-7
Ebook ISBN: 978-0-9861555-7-4

First Printing: February 2016

Contents

Dedication

For Bobbi, my confidant, friend, and mother. She taught me when something is useful, use it; when something is wasteful, chuck it; and when you have a dream, follow it. For if you can't answer the question, "Why not," then there's no reason to ask "Why." And, it's worth doing now.

Introduction

"What have I gotten myself into?"

We've all asked that question. Parents have asked this question. College students have asked it. Entrepreneurs have asked it. Soldiers have asked it as they sweat through basic training.

By the time we get around to asking, "What have I gotten myself into?" we feel overwhelmed, surprised, overworked, underappreciated, and even lost. If you pose the question to friends or colleagues, the answers may range from "A mess!" to "I don't know, what HAVE you gotten yourself into?"—offering neither a solution nor relief.

The realization that we're "in too deep" brings with it additional stress or worry, as well as physical changes, including exhaustion, an inability to think clearly, confusion, and even body aches. Interestingly, these are some of the very same symptoms that are characteristic of dehydration. Even though lack of water is unlikely to be the root of the problem you're facing, the parallels are remarkable. Water is an essential element for life. Without water, the human body will shut down and die. In the same way, we can fail at achieving our goals—or at minimum, experience unnecessary pain—unless we possess or develop certain key elements.

The Here and Now

In today's world, we enjoy efficiencies that didn't exist even two years ago. While this technology should make life easier to navigate, in truth, each new application brings with it an expectation that we can do more with less. Unfortunately, we end up just filling our lives with *more*. So, even with all this "efficient" technology, it is as difficult as ever to spend quality time with our families, enjoy our hobbies, or even learn new skills because rather than being streamlined, we're just plain busy. If you can relate, this book is for you.

When we reach the point of asking, "What have I gotten myself into?" it is far more important to determine what brought us to this feeling of being overwhelmed than it is to answer the question. It is rare, however, that people reflect on the underlying cause of the emotion.

The best place to start the search for relief from stress and busyness is at the precise moment when you ask the question. Reflect upon the events leading up to the moment. In some cases, you will immediately realize that a specific event made you feel empty, overworked, emotionally parched. In other cases, you may recognize that something is missing from your life. In truth, if you have reached the point of depletion, something is *definitely* missing.

Just like water is essential for your physical wellness, five elements are required to ensure that any initiative—or life—is successful:

Information

Planning

Motivation

Support

Leadership

These elements are the five waters of success. When any one of these success principles is lacking, "dehydration" will occur and the initiative will fail. The concept holds true in business, as well as in the challenges we face in our personal lives.

The first element, *information*, can be in the form of facts about the past or future. It can be training or a round-table discussion. It can be received during an interview when we've applied for a new position. It can be in the form of a contract when considering a publisher for a book. When information is lacking, whether it's because someone didn't offer enough information or we didn't ask the right questions, in most situations, it exists somewhere. I'm certainly not trying to sell you on the idea that it's possible to think of every alternative for every situation. I am, instead, a believer that a lack of information is the primary contributor to the overwhelmed feeling we get when we wonder what we have gotten ourselves into.

The second element is *planning*. What happens when we're so excited about an idea that we don't spend enough time planning? Anyone who has ever read a personal development book or article knows the familiar cliché: When you fail to plan, you plan to fail.

Perhaps we have an amazing plan based on plenty of information, but lack the third element: *motivation*. In general, people do things for personal satisfaction. At the core of motivation is the question, "What's in it for me?" For many who volunteer their time to help others, the satisfaction of knowing they are making a difference provides enough motivation to drive through any adversity that will potentially deter them from giving their time. Some take on a new role or position because they are motivated by a pay increase or the potential for gaining more status. Motivation is unique to each person and is driven by personality, culture, society, personal history, future goals, and many other factors.

For the element of *support*, I invite you to reflect on a time when you've thought, "Am I the only one who wants this?" Even though you were carrying out a well thought-out plan with all the information you needed and had all the right motivators in place, the amount (or lack) of support is clearly a crucial element. When more than one individual is included in and affected by the same initiative, lack of support can cause it to fail.

The final element needed for success and clarity when faced with a challenge is *leadership*. Behind every great initiative, be it in the business world, volunteer work, or personal situations, is great leadership. I'm not only talking about the executives, managers, supervisors, and positional leaders. I'm talking about the individuals who offer anything worth repeating. Even among a group of friends, the leader of the group changes regularly. Sometimes it's the one who comes up with the perfect restaurant idea for dinner, or the one who provides comfort to another.

When you combine great leadership with the other elements, you can accomplish amazing, even seemly impossible things. A great leader can identify what motivates each person on their team and, with that awareness, inspire others to tap into and satisfy their personal or professional motivators.

When leaders engage in a well-developed plan, provide accurate and pertinent information, engage others so they are motivated and continually offer support, the initiative will carry so much momentum that it would be nearly impossible for it to fail.

Since you've made it this far in the book, I assume you realize that the concept behind the five waters of success is not rocket science. Nor is it a magic wand that will instantly solve every challenge and prevent you from ever feeling overwhelmed again. Applying these success principles requires work and commitment. But it's their simplicity that makes them effective, applicable, and helpful in any situation. When you are feeling dehydrated and weary, my hope is that you'll use this book to identify and replenish the essential elements that are missing from your life. Drink deeply.

Inspiration

One single event in my life gave me the idea of gathering these five success principles into an organized format. I first shared the ideas presented in *How Much Water Do We Have?* to a close, small group. Their opinions and responses helped me to further develop my thoughts. From there, I presented the message to larger groups. Since then, the message of the five waters of success has spread, and I have heard story after story of people reaching out to others by email or over the phone and with the words, "I need some water over here" or "I have some spare water if anybody needs it."

Later in the book, I'll explain these five waters of success in more detail, but first I want share the true story that gave birth to the idea for *How Much Water Do We Have?*

Section I

How Much Water Do We Have?

Let me set the stage. My wife and I had desk jobs. We each smoked a pack a day. Our idea of exercise was watching extreme diet and exercise programs while eating a bag of chips.

In late June 2011, we were in Eastern Tennessee to celebrate our anniversary. For us, there was no place on Earth as beautiful as the Great Smoky Mountains National Park. And as amateur photographers with new equipment, we were ready for anything. Well, anything except for what actually happened.

We had gotten married in the park two years earlier and had returned two or three times a year since then. Many of the places we had photographed on previous trips were within a short walk from the road. Other places required up to a five-mile round trip hike on fairly level ground. We always took precautions: taking short hikes early in the visit and increasing the distance we ventured away from our vehicle as the week progressed.

On that particular morning, we had no plans and no destination in mind other than to stop at a restaurant for breakfast. We loaded the car with our standard supplies: a small cooler with soft drinks, maps, cigarettes, a first aid kit, books about the waterfalls which included directions to the falls, and elevation maps. We also packed two water bottles each, a water-filled backpack, and of course, our camera equipment. We never knew what kind of specific filter, lens, or tripod we might need at any given location so we packed it all.

My sling-style camera case contained my camera, a 250 mm zoom lens, a macro zoom lens, an external flash, ten filters with lens mount, two different types of lens hoods, a leather case with three more threaded filters, a cleaning kit, a spare pack of cigarettes with a lighter, and a video camera. Thankfully, it had a waist strap for additional support.

Kris toted the backpack, which was similarly well-supplied. It included water in plastic canteens, a waterproof cigarette case, a bear bell, bear mace, and of course, her own spare pack of cigarettes. We also toted hiking poles. She carried one for each side, and I carried just one because I used a full-sized tripod for walking support on the other side. We were ready for almost anything.

It was nearing 10:00 a.m. when we finally got the car loaded, put on our sunglasses, and started down the mountain from our cabin. It was a slow drive to get into Gatlinburg, and at 10:30 a.m., we arrived just in time to get our favorite greasy breakfast sandwiches. We ate them in the car in the restaurant's parking lot because the air conditioner in the car offered much more relief from the already-hot day than the restaurant did. As we pulled away, I hesitated at the edge of Highway 321, looking both ways. Finally, I put the decision in Kris's hands.

"Which way should we go?" I asked.

"We're out by Greenbrier. Let's start there," she replied.

We had been to the Greenbrier area many times in the past. It offers amazing cascades, smooth rocks, cool water and colorful foliage, regardless of the time of year. The scenery from the entrance of the National Park to the end of the paved road changes constantly. The water flow never looks the same twice. Several small, one-lane bridges provide the perfect locations to set up the tripod.

Knowing from previous experience that the area is beautiful year round, I quickly agreed and turned left towards the Greenbrier area of the park. We drove for several miles without saying a word—we were soaking up the scenery and having the time of our lives. It was the first day of our anniversary trip where we could settle into nature and let the stress of our professional lives melt away in the East Tennessee heat.

As I approached the entrance to the park, Kris stared out the window into the woods of the National Park. She broke the easy silence with a simple question:

"How much water do we have?"

"A lot. Why?" I responded.

Still looking out the window, she said, "Let's do Ramsey."

I froze for just a minute, seriously considering her proposal. I knew very little about the Ramsey Cascade except that it was a long-term goal of mine to capture an amazing photograph of the waterfall. I had seen pictures of it and I wanted to take some of my own. I knew that to take my own photographs of it, I would have to hike eight miles, round trip. I knew that the hike was considered *strenuous* on a scale of *easy, moderate, difficult,* and *strenuous.* I also knew that my personal skill level was certainly no higher than *moderate* that specific day and that was being generous. But my desire to see and capture images of Ramsey Cascade outweighed any doubts about whether I had the endurance or skill for the hike. I was in.

We drove over the pitted road, stopping briefly at one of the single-lane bridges to take in the view of the Little Pigeon River and considering the scenes we would attempt to capture after returning from the falls that day. An overpowering feeling of excitement about what we were setting out to accomplish washed over us. Then, five miles into the woods, the rough dirt road ended with the sign: RAMSEY CASCADE TRAILHEAD. My excitement grew as I thought of capturing an amazing photograph of the cascade. I would have been fine to not see Ramsey Cascade for years, until then. With the possibility right in front of me though, I envisioned people buying my print of the waterfall. People all over the world have come to the Great Smoky Mountains National Park and hiked the eight miles to and from Ramsey Cascades, many being local families and day hikers that just enjoy the hiking in the Smokies. The number of photographs of this place on the Internet and in peoples' personal collections was unimaginable. Even the vending machines at the Sugarland's Visitors Center had Ramsey Cascades covering the face of them.

Despite this, I had searched many times for photos of Ramsey and never found any photographs that intimidated me as an amateur photographer. I defined intimidation in a photograph as the ones that I saw and thought to myself "There's no way I could capture an image like that." That's not saying there were not some great photos out there, just none that fell into my intimidation category. I *had* to capture that great photograph of the waterfall.

The First Mile and a Half

'What's it going to be?'

S tanding near the trailhead marker, we enjoyed a cigarette and took turns trying to convince each other that this trek was still a good idea.

"Are we really ready for this?"

"No, but we will be by the time we come back."

"What exactly are we thinking?"

"How far do you think we'll make it?"

"Eight miles is a long way."

"I did this hike about ten years ago. Of course, I was ten years younger and a bit more active at the time," Kris said. "The first mile and a half is an old logging road."

She went on to paint a picture of what we would see on the hike. At the end of the logging road, the trail narrows into what sounded like a path into an enchanted forest.

I couldn't wait to get started, but I still wasn't fully convinced we had the stamina for the trip. I proposed that we agree to hike the first mile and a half and then see how we felt. If we didn't feel like we could make it, there would be no harm in coming back to the car. However, once we entered the enchanted forest, we would be fully committed and would not turn around until we reached the waterfall—no matter what. Even considering the possibility of turning around was difficult for me; I really wanted to capture a great photograph of the falls.

It was almost noon by the time we pulled our gear out of the trunk of the car. Hefting my pack, I began to second-guess the amount of weight that I was getting ready to sling onto my back. I removed several items that suddenly seemed less essential, now that we were embarking on an eight-mile hike. In addition to the backpack, I strapped on a hip pack that held the first-aid kit and two additional water bottles. To distribute the cargo more evenly, Kris strapped the tripod to her backpack which allowed me to carry two hiking poles.

Finally, loaded down with gear and with our hiking poles firmly strapped onto our wrists, we ventured past the sign. We felt good! We laughed at each other's silly quips about nothing in particular as we walked along the old logging road.

Soon our conversation slowed and the sounds of each other's slightly labored breathing replaced our words. I heard Kris take a deep breath, and since I was walking slightly ahead of her, I paused and turned around.

She had stopped hiking to catch her breath. I used the moment to rest my lungs a bit, as well. We looked back down the logging road and could still see the sharp bend in the trail that came just after the footbridge where we had crossed over Ramsey Prong at the trailhead. We had successfully hiked about 300 yards.

Laughing about how out of shape we were, we continued along the logging road. Occasionally, I pulled out the video camera to capture our adventure. The road ran parallel to the river so we stopped to take a few photos or video the tiny cascades that fell over the rocks. We also stopped periodically to drink water, but not too much; we needed that water to last for the full eight miles.

We came to what looked like a dead end with an opening in the undergrowth to the river. I walked up to the edge to find out how to cross it and heard my wife say, "We made it."

I looked around to try to determine where we were supposed to go from there. I saw a little opening in the forest marked by a natural arbor of rhododendron and a sign: RAMSEY CASCADE 2.5. An arrow pointed us toward the enchanted forest. We accomplished our first goal! Proud of our achievement, we took off our backpacks and celebrated our success by snapping pictures of each other standing beside the sign and then smoking a couple of cigarettes with big smiles on our faces.

High-fives aside, we had a decision to make: continue on or turn back.

"How do you feel?" she asked me.

"I feel good. My legs don't hurt like they did when we started, which is weird. I think they were just tight, but loosened up as we went along. How about you?"

"Not bad at all, really. I feel the same way. My legs loosened up. They feel a little tingly, but I think that's just from using them more than usual."

While we rested, several people walked past us. A few couples chose this sign as the point to turn around and head back to the trailhead. Some held hands as if they were out for an easy stroll.

My wife asked me what I wanted to do. We were nearly halfway to Ramsey and, based on the first mile and a half, I told her I thought I could go on another ten miles. "It gets more difficult after this," she warned.

She explained that the narrower trail would be marked with roots and rocks that we would have to step over. She also warned me that the climb would be more strenuous than what we just completed. She described how, on her earlier hike, part of the trail seemed eerily quiet, and then, just about the time she thought she missed it or that she was never going to find it, she heard the rushing water again and saw the waterfall. She couldn't wait for me to see it and to capture a photograph that portrayed the size and beauty of the falls. It was a warning mixed with enticement, one she ended by asking me, "What's it going to be?"

I thought about the photos I had seen of the waterfall. I thought about the opportunity that awaited two and a half miles in front of me. I thought of taking a photo—perhaps one of the greatest representations of Ramsey Cascades—and how it might launch my hobby into a career.

I don't know how long I stood there thinking, but when she asked again, I responded, "I say we go on."

With that, we stood up, put on our packs, took deep breaths, and looked at each other. With a smile on her face, she said, "Ready?"

"No turning back, right?" I said. She agreed and we took our first steps through the arbor of rhododendron unaware that the next two and a half miles would change our lives.

The Tulip Tree

'The last photograph we took on our hike to Ramsey Cascade.'

The next part of the hike was breathtakingly beautiful. Rhododendron bloomed all around us and we could hear the rushing water to our right.

We hiked the gradual incline for about half of an hour before Kris stopped to catch her breath. It was definitely time to drink water. We rested for two to three minutes before moving again.

As we traveled further along the trail, the incline increased. The trail also became more difficult to navigate. It seemed as though no single step was level with the last, and between each step, tree roots snaked across the path threatening our footing. I kept looking back to check on my wife and saw sweat rolling down her face. It was time to stop, catch our breath, and drink a little more water. We sipped only what was needed to eliminate stomach cramps and then continued.

Each step seemed to take us farther away from the river. When the trail weaved back towards the water, we saw that we were on top of a fifty-foot cliff. Again, we stopped, longer this time. In fact, after every five minutes of progress, we rested for three to five minutes.

Finally, we reached a river crossing. Stepping onto the narrow bridge, I took hold of the handrail and crossed easily. I took a few steps up the trail on the other side before looking back at Kris.

My wife, who is afraid of heights, stopped before the bridge, weary and out of breath. Eight feet below, the river rushed under the bridge. Actually, the term bridge was generous. It wasn't really a bridge at all but a twelve-inch diameter tree that had been cut lengthwise and laid over the river. Several beams, which were made of smaller tree trunks, lined up alongside the log to serve as a makeshift handrail for the bridge that spanned the twenty-foot crossing. At five feet, three inches tall, Kris knew she would have to balance the beam while leaning to her right to grab the handrail to cross the river.

"I don't think I can do this, honey," she said to me.

I stepped back across the bridge and encouraged her, "Keep your focus across the bridge. Keep your eye on the level ground on the other side and walk across it." I continued by explaining that when we walk normally on level ground, our steps do not reach wider than the width of the wooden crossing and that the apparent narrowness was an illusion.

"Stay focused and just walk across like this." I kept my focus straight across the beam and walked across without hesitation. When I turned back this time, I could see a hint of exhaustion in her face, and, more prevalent, fear. She stepped carefully on the beam and, looking down at her grounded foot, tried to determine where to place her hiking poles.

"Forget the poles," I called out. "Just strap them to your wrists and balance with your hands. You can reach the railing, but it's going to feel off balance."

She stared down at the river. For the first time, I noticed the intensity of the rushing water below. If she fell, she would be swept 50 yards down river within seconds... if she didn't get caught up on the rocks.

"Look at me, sweetheart," I told her. "Put your other foot on the beam and look at me. You can do this. You are going to do this. Do not let the fear keep you on the other side of the bridge."

She pulled herself up onto the beam and leaned out for the handrail. Her legs began to shake, but she took another step. She looked up at me, then down to the rushing water again. I could tell she felt dizzy from the other side where I was standing.

"Look up at me or focus just on the board," I shouted. "The water doesn't exist. It's just you and the board."

She took another step, then another, and another. Her progression was gradual and shaky. I stood watching, paralyzed with the knowledge that, if she slipped, any action I took would be too late. I watched powerlessly as she grasped the rail with both hands and continued to shuffle along the board without ever crossing one foot over the other. Finally, she reached out to me with one hand still on the railing. Grabbing hold of my hand, she jumped to solid ground.

Still shaking and looking back at the crossing, she simply said, "I did it."

As we walked along the trail together, she said, "You just don't understand what that feels like—that kind of fear." I listened as she described how the fear took possession of her. Her legs began to shake, followed by her hips and torso, until her entire body trembled uncontrollably at the thought of falling. Standing on the other side of the bridge that day, she'd felt as if her body had betrayed her. Her conscious mind told her to cross the bridge, but her feet had refused to move. Falling into the rushing water below seemed unlikely after watching me cross so easily, but that didn't matter to the irrational fear that gripped her.

The river floated along to our left now and we had plenty of time to watch it since we stopped to rest every few minutes of hiking. We knew that stopping so often only made things worse—our muscles cooled and tightened each time we rested—but with the incline, our out-of-shape legs and lungs demanded a break. I also noticed we drank a little more water each time we stopped and were just getting to the bottom of our first canteens.

We rounded a bend to the left and stopped just before another water crossing. I crossed and then stopped on the other side to wait for Kris. This bridge wasn't as high as before; it was shorter but wider in girth, and the handrailing was straighter. My wife didn't hesitate. She stepped right up and crossed.

The trail leveled off a bit to a twenty-degree incline (an improvement over what we'd been climbing) and took us farther away from the water. Although it wasn't flat, the path was wider and smoother with more dirt and fewer rocks and roots. The hiking should have been easier. Unfortunately, the ability to take longer strides increased the pain in our legs.

We were able to hike for ten minutes at a time on that stretch of the trail before stopping for another two minutes. Sipping now from our second canteens of water, we knew we had a long way to go, so we drank less each time to conserve our supply. After one short break, I put away my canteen and started moving again before hearing my wife say, "Wait another minute, please."

When I looked back, I saw her trying to rub a cramp out of her calf muscles. I showed her how to stretch her calf muscles with lunges. She winced with each leg, but it seemed to help.

On the trail ahead, we saw people laughing and taking pictures of each other in front of us. For a minute, I thought—hoped—we had arrived at the waterfall.

As we reached the other hikers, one was explaining to the other that the tree in front of them was the sixth largest tulip tree in the park. It was huge—the biggest tree I had ever seen. And, it provided another great place to stop for a break. This time, we took off our backpacks and stayed for more than five minutes.

Standing by the tree, I suddenly realized I hadn't taken any photographs since the few at the beginning of the trail. I got my camera out and took a few photos of the tree, but there was no way to tell just how big the tree was without something to compare for scale. So, I asked my wife if she would take a picture of me standing in front of the tree so that people could tell just how big it was. She was more than willing, since doing so meant she could rest her legs a little longer.

It was the last photograph we took on our hike up to Ramsey Cascade.

About a Mile

'You're getting really close.'

As we started on our way again, the intense pain in our legs told us the break we had just taken was far too long. The trail itself didn't do us any favors. The smooth dirt and gentle incline gave way to a steep, treacherous path crisscrossed with roots as big as small trees. The roots stretched across the trail like thousands of snakes in search of food. The rocks that littered the trail were so large that we had to extend our legs across them, step up on them, or go around them. All the obstacles increased the number of steps we had to take to go the same distance as we had up to that point.

We couldn't hike more than twenty feet at a time without becoming winded and stopping for another minute. Many times, the incline was so steep that erosion caused us to step up sixteen inches to navigate the trail. At each similar step, I went first, turned around and braced one arm around a tree as I reached out the other to grasp Kris's hand to pull her up to the next level.

We saw a couple returning from the waterfall so I asked them "How much farther do we have?" The man replied, "It's about a mile."

Just one mile away! One single mile from one of my greatest opportunities as a photographer. I thought about how many miles my feet had taken me and kept telling myself, "One more mile."

We continued hiking short distances at a time. Too winded to speak, we just looked each time we stopped as if to say, "You all right?"

As I watched her hike, I could see that each step brought my wife excruciating pain. I asked her how much she hurt. She told me that stepping down didn't hurt at all. The pain came each time she lifted her foot off the ground to take another step, and then it eased again when she returned her foot to the ground. "Every time I lift my foot to take another step, my leg cramps up," she said rubbing her calf muscles. Every step brought the sensation of a charley horse.

I didn't like to see her in pain, but something else had me worried. The air was cooler, so she wasn't sweating; although to touch her skin felt like she was on fire from the inside. Her skin was red and blotchy. I told her to drink more water, but she was concerned that I wouldn't have enough when I needed it. I insisted that I had plenty of water left and she should drink whatever she felt she needed. She put her canteen away and said, "Come on, let's go."

We continued for what seemed like an hour or more and met more people on their way back down the mountain. I knew we had to be getting close! I asked them how much farther it was to the waterfall.

They stopped in the trail, turned to each other and mumbled something to themselves until they agreed upon a response. They nodded their heads and one of the gentleman in the group finally said in a very encouraging tone, "You're getting really close. It's about a mile."

Fifteen Minutes

'A huge wall of water....'

Kris's shoulders dropped. "I really want you to see it," she said. "It's really a beautiful waterfall."

"I'm going to see it, and so are you."

The difficulty of the trail hadn't improved. All we could do was hike, take a break, catch our breath, drink some water, and repeat.

One step after another, we continued for another forty-five minutes before we crossed paths with another couple.

"How much farther is it from here?" I asked them.

The woman replied with, "You have about thirty minutes to reach the waterfall," then turned to her husband for confirmation.

He nodded his head and said, "That's probably about right. It's thirty minutes, but it gets much steeper and much more rocky.

"How much steeper and rockier can it get?"

We received no response from our inquiry. I turned to my wife and said, "We're getting close, really close."

"I don't think I have another thirty minutes in me, honey," she said. "I just don't think I can do it."

Unwilling to quit, I said "Let's take one last good break before we finish this, because we are going to finish this."

Kris didn't think she could make it, but she wanted me to see the waterfall. "How much water do you have?" she asked. "Do you have enough to go the rest of the way?"

"It's fine," I said as I helped her remove her backpack. "Drink some more."

Without the weight of her heavy pack, she seemed quite refreshed but was still not convinced that she could continue. I reached down to the ground to pick up her water-filled backpack with the tripod strapped across the back and slung it over my shoulder.

"What are you doing?" she asked.

"I'm hiking. I'm going to see that waterfall. We made a deal that, if we entered the enchanted forest, we were not turning back—no matter what."

"You're not going to carry my pack," she protested. Instead of arguing, I turned around and started climbing between rocks as big as houses. "Catch me and you can have it back."

The lack of weight on her back allowed Kris to maneuver the trail more easily; a good thing, since the gentleman we had spoken to last was right. The incline increased to more than forty-five degrees and the rocks seemed unavoidable.

My legs began to fail me. My weakened muscles didn't hurt as much during that stretch of the hike because they were numb. I couldn't feel the strain of each step anymore, nor could I tell when my foot touched the ground or when it was time to shift my weight to take the next step. Lightheaded, I felt an ache grow in the back of my head.

We stopped for a break, and I took some aspirin out of my hip pack and drank it down with some water. We stayed right there for just a minute looking around. An eerie quietness surrounded us. No birds chirped, and we couldn't hear the sound of the rushing river that had accompanied us much of the way. A slight breeze offered an energizing relief from the late June heat.

When we started walking again, we were faced with climbing between giant boulders that lined each side of the rocky trail. Navigating the narrow space between the two twenty-foot-high rocks challenged us in a new way. I had to keep facing forward because the width of the water-filled pack in addition to my own backpack wouldn't allow me to fit through sideways. That would have been fine except some of the steps we had to take were two feet or higher. With my numbed legs, I stepped forward—and up—while Kris pushed my backpack up to assist me. Then, I reached back and offered her my hand to pull her up.

Finally, above the rocks, the trail became less of an incline. We continued on for a quarter mile or so when I turned to her and quietly said, "Stop."

We looked at each other for a moment. There were still very few sounds. We heard our own breathing, the shuffling of our feet as we shifted our weight and turned to find the source of the other noise we heard. It was faint and barely audible, but it was real. We smiled at each other as we listened to the distant sound of rushing water— the unmistakable roar of the falls.

We both sighed deeply, turned toward the sound, and focused all of our attention on the last stretch of that hike. We knew we were heading in the right direction because the roar kept getting louder.

I walked ahead of Kris, farther than I had all day, until I reached a shallow stream of water. I turned around and asked, "Now what?"

She laughed and replied, "Go across it."

I had barely crossed the small creek when my heart began to race at the sight before me. I gasped for air, put my hand over my mouth, and exclaimed, "I see it!"

"What do you see?" she asked.

"It's just a huge wall of water!"

I hesitated briefly to help her across the creek. With a burst of energy, we hiked together. As we neared the falls, the trees, underbrush, rocks, and rhododendron became sparser revealing more of the view. As we stepped out of the woods, we found a large rock near the edge of the falls. Standing there, with the mist rushing toward us, we held hands and stared tear-filled eyes at the 120-foot waterfall. White water danced from level to level prancing across the rocks until it rushed past us just to our right.

"It's close to 5:30. You have fifteen minutes to capture this," Kris said.

Four More Miles

'About half.'

We had been caught deep in the park after dark before, an experience neither of us wanted to repeat. Although the sun hadn't technically set, the mountains surrounded us, blocking out much of the late-afternoon light. In my head, I calculated the remaining daylight based on the time it took us to get to the waterfall. Understanding that our hike was only half way complete, I knew that fifteen minutes was a generous offer.

I snapped a variety of shots using different filters and settings as quickly as I could. I didn't want to get back home, download the photos, and determine that none of them was very good, so I was cautious to make sure every setting was just right. After the series of more than sixty photographs, I put the equipment away and walked over to my wife to carry out one of our traditions. Without cameras or tripods, we stood hand-in-hand simply enjoying the scene in front of us. Some moments can only be captured within the heart.

Though no less painful, the return hike was much faster than the hike to the falls. We used a different set of muscles to go downhill than those we used going up the mountain. Rather than sore calf muscles, we experienced shin splints that started just after climbing down between the boulders and continued for the next three and three quarter miles. During the return hike, we didn't have much strength to stop our momentum down the steep slope and, on occasion, would have to reach out to a tree or slide down with our feet until we stopped on a root crossing the trail.

It seemed as though we were the only ones left on the mountain. At one point, we found a broken pair of flip-flops which brought two thoughts into our minds. First was that of how unlucky one would be to lose their flip-flop with so much farther to go. The second was that of wonderment as to why someone would hike eight miles round trip in flip-flops in the first place.

Nearly a quarter of a mile down, we crossed paths with a family with two small children. All of them were barefoot and stepping gingerly. We asked if there was anything we could do to help, but they insisted that they were fine. The children danced around each other as though they had never worn shoes a day in their lives. Their dad laughed and said, "My flip-flop had a blowout back there a ways, but it's all right; we can make it. We don't wear shoes much anyway."

We continued down the trail without speaking much. Instead, we listened to each other's vocal indications of discomfort. We passed the place where the steps were eighteen inches down. We passed the tulip trees and crossed the bridges. The further we walked, the worse we felt. Every step brought incredibly intense pain to our thighs, calves, and shins. Even our toes hurt from being jammed into the front of our shoes with each step of the downhill slope.

Most of the hike down was a blur in our minds. We just wanted to be at the bottom of the mountain, at times wishing we could just duck our heads and roll the rest of the way down.

We reached the opening of the enchanted forest, which we now thought of as the gate to the trail of terror. The last mile and a half, though still downhill, felt much less strenuous only because it didn't require us to lift our feet much more than usual.

Our legs, from our knees down, were completely numb by that point. We could not feel our feet touching the ground at all. Putting one foot in front of the other was more of a fluid impulse of momentum than a purposeful motion. We reached a bend in the path to the left and crossed the footbridge at the trailhead.

There was no excitement or celebration when we arrived at the car around 7:20.

Resting in the car, we reflected on the afternoon with gratitude. "Thank you," Kris said.

"What for?" I asked.

"For not leaving me. I could not have done it without you. I was so scared on that bridge. I swear I was going to turn back when we got to the big rocks. I can't believe you took my pack."

"Thank you for seeing it through," I said. "I was ready to come back with you if you didn't finish. We were either going to finish together or come back together."

"Do you think you got any good shots," she asked me.

"I have no idea, but I do know I'm hungry."

"Me, too. We just did an eight-mile round trip hike on fast-food breakfast. I just want to get back to the cabin and sit in the hot tub. I'm not moving for days."

"I don't think we'll be able to," I said with a half-laugh.

"How much water do we have?" she asked.

I picked up each canteen and the water-filled backpack to check. Knowing we had just experienced many signs of dehydration over the last eight hours, I shook my head in disappointment and embarrassment when I answered her.

"About half."

Section II

The 5 Waters of Success

For the next three days, we went to vehicle-friendly places in the park; primarily the Motor Nature Trail and Cades Cove. The pain in our legs felt incomparable to anything I had experienced before and walking seemed to be the only way to relieve it. By the fourth day, we were hiking again and photographing more wonderful places, like Mouse Creek Falls and Midnight Hole, which are both in the Big Creek area of the park.

We recalled our Ramsey Cascade adventure throughout the week, replaying nearly every step. My thoughts kept returning to the most basic cause of our agonizing experience, dehydration. According to MedicineNet.com, some of the symptoms of dehydration are:

- Thirst
- Clammy skin
- Decreased sweating

- Increased breathing rate
- Decreased urine production
- Weakness
- Muscle cramps
- Severe headaches

Water has sometimes been referred to as the element that brings life because, without it, the human body would not survive. In this book, water is a metaphor for all the things that an individual or an organization needs when faced with some type of change or new initiative. Those things include having the right information, planning, motivation, support, and leadership.

Information

From the time I was a Boy Scout, I learned lessons primarily from experiencing bad situations. In the early 1980s, I was in Troop 44 from Lititz, Pennsylvania. Under the leadership of a great scoutmaster, I learned about the heart of the "Be Prepared" motto. He taught us that we needed to be prepared, mentally and physically, for any conditions we might face. That preparation began with gathering information. My scoutmaster was a great source of information. For example, he told us we should dress in layers while hiking, particularly in the wintertime, since the activity would warm us up. Layers would allow us to stay comfortable. He also told us, repeatedly, to pack extra socks since you never knew when your feet might get wet on a hike. I respected the scoutmaster and knew the information he was sharing was important, but, having not yet faced those situations, I had no real reason to remember that important information—that is, until our troop went on a winter campout.

Planning

Every year, the troop participated in a Klondike derby where we built a sled and stopped at different stations to compete against other troops. We completed a variety of tasks, from building a fire without the aid of matches or a lighter, to properly diagnosing and treating an injured person using only items that we carried with us.

The day was full of events and adventures, but by 2:00 in the afternoon, I was sitting in a sleeping bag in my tent waiting for my socks, which were hung by the fire, to dry out. Sitting in a cozy tent might not sound all that bad, but for me, it felt like torture. I was miserable because I wasn't out there helping to support the rest of my troop in the derby. Thinking back on the information the scoutmaster gave me, I realized I was missing all of the fun because I didn't plan properly. I wasn't prepared. I didn't bring an extra pair of socks. I asked the scoutmaster if I could just borrow somebody else's spare pair of socks, but he refused to allow it, insisting that the experience would certainly help me remember to pack an extra pair of socks next time. It wasn't only cold, wet feet that helped me learn that lesson. The response I got from the others when they returned to camp made me acutely aware of the consequences of my unpreparedness. Nobody protected me from hearing the other boys' wonderful stories of fun. And some of the scouts went out of their way to ensure I was aware of their disapproval.

I learned the lesson. As an adult, I have traveled quite a bit for my career, and there has not been one time that I have used all the socks I have packed for the trip.

Motivation

I've also learned some important lessons while in the Army. The first was about motivation and came during basic training. In preparation for a course my platoon had to complete, we shouted rehearsed statements in unison to show the drill sergeants that we were ready for the upcoming task. One drill sergeant would shout, "Are you motivated?" and in perfect unison we would give the response, "Motivated, motivated, always motivated!"

When we finished our perfect response, the drill sergeant said, "No you're not. You respond that way because I told you to respond that way. You want to complete the next task because I told you that you have to complete it. The problem is that you don't want to complete it for yourself; you want to because I told you to and that's not enough today."

He explained that to get through this next challenge, each of us had to want to complete it for ourselves and for the people standing next to us. He said, "If you only want this because I told you to, you will never get through it. Imagine yourself at the end of it. Close your eyes and see yourself celebrating today's victory. Now get through this course because you want to feel that way, not because I told you to."

Our platoon was better than any other on the course that day because he helped us find our own motivation.

Support

Support is such a strong element of success that when an initiative is lacking the other elements, the right support alone may empower us to see a challenge to completion. The hike to Ramsey Cascade is one personal example of how support empowered the achievement of a goal—despite a serious lack of information and poor planning.

Leadership

Another key lesson I learned from the Army came shortly after transitioning from the regular Army to the Indiana National Guard. I always showed up with perfectly shined boots and a distinctly creased uniform. As I looked around at others, I noticed that I looked better than everyone else. Some showed up without any polish on their boots at all, and their uniform looked as if they just picked it up from the floor in the corner of the closet because that's where they threw it last month. Over time, I relaxed my uniform routine. Instead of worrying about perfection, I just did a quick boot shine and made sure to carefully hang my clean uniform so that the pants and shirt would get a natural crease. I still looked better than most of my fellow soldiers.

One specific Saturday morning, I showed up and reported as usual to the master sergeant. She gave me information regarding the weekend and then pointed out that I used to show up every month with perfectly-shined boots and a pressed uniform. She asked, "Why don't you do that anymore?" I explained that I had noticed the standard in the National Guard was not as high as the standard in the Army, so I didn't spend as much time on my uniform as I used to. She stood up from behind her desk and shouted, "That's the worst excuse I've ever heard in my life. You set your own standard, and I can clearly see what yours has become."

That was fifteen years ago and there's not a single day that goes by that I don't take a few seconds to look in the mirror before leaving my house so that I can answer the question, "What is my standard today?"

In addition to helping you understand these five life-giving elements, this book will provide an opportunity for personal reflection. Regardless of your current title, or whether you are part of an organization of volunteers, or have a paying job, it is likely you have either faced or are currently facing some type of change or initiative. Maybe you have a personal goal you want to accomplish, such as going back to school, learning a new trade, or going on a hike to a place you've never been before. Perhaps, you are experiencing adversity in your personal life.

Take a moment to think about a specific challenge you are currently facing. Write down this challenge to keep it at the forefront of your mind while you're reading. (If you are reading this in a print format, a space has been included on the next page. If you are reading it on a tablet or computer, use the annotation tools to record the challenge you have selected.) Take a moment to do this before continuing to the next page.

At the end of each section, there will be questions for reflection. As you consider your response, think specifically about this challenge.

The challenge I'm facing is....

_____

_____

_____

_____

_____

_____

_____

_____

_____

_____

_____

_____

_____

_____

Information

'An elementary answer....'

The Hike

My wife had done the hike before, but it had been ten years prior. Aside from the fact that her fitness level had declined during those ten years, over time, she had forgotten the details of the hike and focused entirely on the beauty of the waterfall.

The first time we looked at the Ramsey Cascades Elevation Map (*Figure 1*) was the day *after* the hike. At the time, we were trying to determine why the hike was so much more difficult for us than it was for the others on the trail.

The information on the map would have been extremely useful to have before the hike. Did this map even exist? Of course it did; we just didn't look at it. In fact, a version of the elevation map was in one of the waterfall books we had brought with us (and left in the car without looking at it). I'm also certain we were not the first people to go on the hike. We watched people all day returning from the waterfall, but it

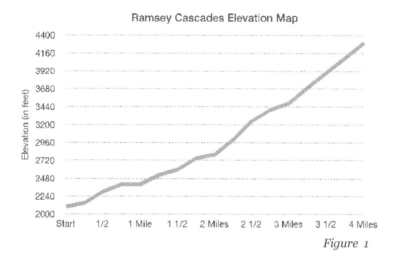

Figure 1

wasn't until we were well into the hike that we thought to ask what kind of terrain lay ahead of us. We might have taken different precautions or even returned to the car if we had taken advantage of all the information available to us. If we had asked some questions beforehand, we would not have become dehydrated.

Along with not looking at the elevation map, we were also lacking the knowledge about the number of obstacles, such as roots and boulders. When we were at the bridge where fear threatened to send Kris back to the car, I suddenly realized that just because a person had done something ten years prior does not mean that they remember all the pertinent information required to accomplish it again. Had she remembered that particular bridge earlier, Kris would have had the opportunity to mentally prepare for the crossing.

The Real World

Having enough accurate information is, quite possibly, the most important aspect of a change; it is necessary at every stage of a transition. Initially, the information needed is an evaluation of both the current state and the end state. In other words, where are you now and where do you want to be?

The errors we made due to lack of information can happen in any organization. When people facing a change have previously experienced something similar, they will reflect on their prior experience to prepare themselves for the upcoming change.

Some people will remember only the positive, while others remember only the negative. During our hike to Ramsey Cascade, we focused entirely on the waterfall and on capturing a great photograph without any consideration of the difficulty of the hike. You may have experienced the same phenomena. When you've accomplished a goal, it's easy to forget or gloss over the challenges and focus on the achievement.

Starting something with an overly positive (or negative) perspective puts you at a disadvantage that may lead to doubt as the initiative progresses. As emotional discomfort or physical pain sets in, the people involved may question the accuracy and/or quantity of the information they received. They'll wonder whether they have what it takes to continue and succeed.

That's exactly what happened when my wife came to that footbridge. She felt terrified at the prospect of crossing the bridge and really wanted to turn around. There may be times in your own journey when you are presented with a challenge that makes you question whether you can continue. This test of fear or self-doubt is when some people quit. I'm betting that you don't want to quit, which makes having the right information all the more important.

So how do you know if you have a sufficient amount of information to face a challenge? The answer may seem elementary: Ask the right questions.

Who? What? Where? When? Why?

Start with the basics and ask the following questions to figure out where you are (current state) and what it will take to get where you want to go (end state).

Who is involved?

What is the goal?

Where will the event take place?

When will the goal be reached?

When should the initiative begin?

Ask "why?" repeatedly during this discovery process to ensure each action and decision is purposeful and moves you toward your goal. This should also be the question asked whenever you experience a marked success or a setback. Understanding why you've made progress provides the opportunity to repeat the actions that enabled you to advance toward your goal. Likewise, when you experience a setback, determining why—what caused it—allows you to adjust your actions and reduce setbacks going forward.

My Dad used to share a story with me whenever something I attempted didn't go well. The story he told was that of a farmer whose cow was stuck in a ditch. He told me that the farmer only needed three things to correct the problem. First, get the cow out of the ditch. Second, determine how the cow got into the ditch, and, third, ensure the cow never falls in the ditch again. The military calls that process an AAR or After Action Review. It's a simple evaluation that allows you to keep doing what went well and correct the things that didn't.

The collection of accurate information is important for several reasons. The first reason is to create personal initiative. Some people are more likely to engage in activities surrounding the goal when they have been provided with plenty of information. Those who have personal initiative require less repeated communication from decision makers as the information has helped create a vision for the future.

Many times, individuals or groups initiate change with just enough information to get started. Even if you don't have all the information you need or want to know, you must know two things to successfully move forward: What is the goal and Why is it a goal? If you're working with a team, your team members need to know the answers to those two essential questions.

Accurate and Timely

If you are a leader, it is important to ensure that you are distributing information to your team consistently and accurately. The fact that information is available does not mean everyone is aware of it. That was certainly the case with Kris and me. Plenty of information existed about the elevation and terrain of the Ramsey Cascade hike. But we hadn't found it yet. Even worse, we chose not to look for it.

As a leader, it's your responsibility to make sure your entire team has all the information they need to succeed. Unfortunately, it's quite common for leaders to forget to share information. When that happens, team members end up with conflicting information. This truth begs the question, if the information doesn't come from you, where do your team members get the inaccurate intel? Often times, they make it up. Really. People tell themselves stories to fill in areas that are unclear to them for when they don't receive information directly from a reliable source. As long as their artificial version of the information seems logical, they believe this information to be the truth. Then they share it with others to ensure everyone has the same information. Sharing gives them a sense of purpose and pride in the fact that they were able to "help" somebody else.

The truth is, as a leader, you face some unique challenges. In many cases, you'll have much more information than the people who are most directly affected. For example, as a leader of your family, you probably don't tell your kids everything about the decisions that affect where and how they live. You deliver it on a need-to-know basis. The same is true in business; some information affects only certain individuals. Leaders have to decide which (and how much) information each person needs and then ensure they have it. At the same time, leaders need to be acutely aware of the risks and prevalence of misinformation. Know, too, that for every layer of leadership in your organization, there exists an equal number of possibilities for misinformation.

The timing of sharing information can also be very important. For instance, if you are caring for an elderly parent who is in poor health, you may need to gather information from a variety of sources before sharing the information with that parent. You'll need to speak to doctors to determine the severity of the injury or illness. You'll need to know whether physical therapy is involved in the recovery and, if so, how much rehabilitation will be required for full recovery. The likelihood of full recovery should also be discussed. Doctors and people closest to the patient can answer questions regarding their emotional state and mental health. Alternative living conditions may need to be considered, which may mean gathering information about assisted living facilities, nursing homes, and home health care programs in the event full recovery is not reached.

As the information is gathered, the timing of when to share the collected information with your aging parent can be very delicate. If it's provided too early, it could create more confusion or stress. If it's provided too late, it could have lasting effects on their recovery. Because of the sensitive nature of when to share the information, be aware that some information may need to be shared quickly while other facts may need to be purposely withheld until the time is right.

Whether the situation is an unhealthy person or the strategic positioning of an organization, leaders must be fully aware of what information has been withheld and why. If there is no significant reason for not sharing information, consider the benefits of allowing others being "in the know." One chief benefit is that well-informed people are equipped to carry out the work and make adjustments when unexpected success or setbacks occur—with less need to re-engage the leader.

Ask the Right Questions—Use the Best Sources

Earlier in this chapter, I provided a list of basic questions to ask when you start any new goal or endeavor. Knowing the right questions to ask is important. But it's equally important to gather information from the best sources. Choosing the right person or people from whom to gather information is also essential.

Who has the answers you need? Start with people who have already been successful in similar ventures. Not only will they have the answers to your questions, they'll be able to tell you what other questions you need to ask—questions you may never have thought of on your own.

Not being afraid to ask questions will help you discover what you need to know—and what additional questions you need to ask. Having the attitude of a learner, rather than that of an expert, enables you to continually grow. One example of how that lesson has served me well occurred early in my adult life. When I moved into my first apartment, I built much of my own furniture, including end tables, lamps, and a dining room table. I shared my handiwork with many of my friends, one of whom asked if I would be willing to refinish a table that had been in her family for many years. The tabletop was pitted and scratched and badly in need of some attention. I gladly accepted the challenge.

On my way to the store for supplies for the project, I stopped by my parents' house and asked my mom if she'd like to go with me. She asked what I was buying. I told her, "I need some stain, gloves, brushes, rags, and a plastic tarp."

We walked through the store, checking off every item on the list.

"I think that's everything," Mom said.

I hesitated, then grinned at her and told her I needed just one more item: a book on how to refinish furniture.

I'd stained new furniture before, so I already had some of the information I needed for the project. But having never stripped and refinished furniture before, I felt certain I would have questions about the process—questions I didn't know to ask yet. But I knew the answers would be in that book.

To be successful, every task—new, ongoing, or old—must be supported by timely and accurate information. Just as dehydration occurs when the body doesn't have enough water in the body, lack of information can cause any initiative to fail.

Information
Reflection Questions

Think about the challenge you identified on page 36 as you answer the following questions.

Individual Reflection

What information do I have?

What information do I need before I start or continue?

What information would I like to have that will be helpful?

If others are involved, do I have information they might benefit from?

Leadership Reflection

What information does my staff need to continue with little direction?

What information does my staff already have?

Is the information my staff has accurate?

How much information should I give my staff?

If I'm withholding information, why?

Who needs more information?

When should I deliver that information?

Planning

'The water you drink today will save your life tomorrow.'

The Hike

I'll start with the obvious statement: We should not have attempted an eight-mile hike on a whim. We truly didn't have plans or intentions that morning of hiking a strenuous distance. The conversation that June morning should have played out similar to this:

"How much water do we have?"

"A lot, why?"

"Let's do Ramsey."

"I would love to, but water isn't the deciding factor here. We really need to plan for a hike like that."

Then we wouldn't have felt all the effects of dehydration; we would have had a whole lot more fun the rest of the week and wouldn't have been in so much pain. That said, had the trip been well planned, you would not be reading this book right now either.

When I got out of the Army, I swore I would never run again unless something was chasing me and, believe me, I've stuck to that promise. At the time of the hike, I had worked a desk job for thirteen years. The only exercise I did was yard work and chores, which is nothing like a formal exercise routine. We would have had more success—and less pain—on that vacation if we had repeated our actions of previous trips to the Smokies. Those far more enjoyable trips began with driving along scenic routes that had a few stops where we could get out and walk around. Two or three days later, after building up a little stamina, we would take purposeful hikes where we knew the terrain and elevation ahead of time. Alternatively, we could have prepared our bodies by going on one or two smaller hikes each day for the first three days and then hike to Ramsey Cascades on the fourth day. Both of those options would have been examples of good *planning* for the hike.

The Real World

While I was in the Army, I was stationed at Fort Bliss in El Paso, Texas. It is hot there most of the year, so to ensure our safety, the non-commissioned and commissioned officers reminded us regularly to drink water. We often heard them say, "Even if you're not thirsty, drink. The water you drink today will save your life tomorrow." I believe that statement to be the single most accurate analogy representing the importance of planning.

Planning can either follow the gathering of information or coincide with it. The information gathered is the answer to "What am I getting myself into?" Planning is the answer to the questions: "How do I make this a success?" and "How do I get there?"

We make plans for simple things all the time without recognizing those decisions as plans. A few examples are setting an alarm at night, programming a coffee pot to automatically start brewing fifteen minutes before you wake up, or spending a few minutes in the evening setting out clothes to wear the next day. These are examples of a plan based on the goal of having an efficient morning routine.

Another example of a plan is an action I take when I prepare to travel. Every time I go on a road trip, I gather several pieces of information before departure. Considering my destination, I think about what clothing I need to pack. I review the condition of the vehicle I'll be driving and determine whether it needs an oil change or to have the tires aligned or replaced. I fill up the gas tank either the night before my departure or make the gas station my first stop on the journey. The planning process doesn't stop there. Throughout the trip, I monitor my vehicle's gauges. When the gas gauge dips below half a tank, I start looking for signs that let me know which exits have gas stations and how far down the road they are. I gather all of this information so I can both monitor my plan and be prepared to adjust it at any time.

In other situations, the planning process is much more formal. It begins as soon as you identify a specific goal and determine what it will take to successfully reach that goal.

The information gathering questions you'll need to answer vary based on what the goal is. For example, the questions that need to be answered will be very different for a person or group of people going on a hike than they would be if an organization has a goal to reach record high sales. Different still would be the questions one would need to ask after a surgery if the goal is to walk again.

In each case, though, the questions you'll begin with are Who? What? Where? When? and Why? With that information, you can create the necessary plan(s).

When it comes to formulating a plan, however, there is only one question to ask: How?

Who? What? Where? When? Why? Again?

Even though "How?" is a single question, the five fundamental questions are also involved in deciding how you will accomplish your goal. During the initial process of gathering information, only the current state and end state are considered: where we are now and where we want to be.

To develop a thorough plan, you must answer additional questions.

- What strengths are needed to reach the goal?
- Who possesses those strengths?
- Where do they fit into the goal?
- When should each person begin?
- Why have they been selected?
- What task will each person carry out?

I am one of six training managers working for a large corporation. Each of us has a staff and a portion of the responsibility for the company's national training program.

Recently, my boss asked my opinion on a topic that was being discussed at the executive level. The company's leaders were preparing to initiate a change and she wanted to know how the changes might affect the staff in the field. After asking a few questions to better understand the changes, I suggested that a brief training session would be required to ensure everyone in the field had a general awareness of the plan. In addition to informing the field, the training sessions would prepare the staff to respond to client inquiries and, thus, ensure a positive client experience. She agreed with my assessment and requested that I take on the project.

Being in the process of writing this book, I was hyper-aware of the elements required for successful execution of the training. I began to ask questions to gather information so that I could formulate a plan. Who is affected internally? Who is affected externally? What are the details of the initiative? From a business perspective, why are we doing this? Finally, I asked her, "When is this happening?"

"Next Tuesday," she said.

I requested clarification from her to ensure I was getting the most accurate information possible to set up a successful training session. "This coming Tuesday?" I asked. "A week from today?"

She confirmed the date. I reminded her that Monday was a holiday and asked one more clarifying question.

"Since this is happening on Tuesday, all employees in the country need to be trained by the end of the day this Friday." Again, she confirmed the information and referred me to the project manager.

I happened to know the project manager and sent an email right away to request a meeting. She was in meetings the rest of the day, but was available Wednesday morning. I booked the appointment time, and she sent me a draft of the initiative that wouldn't be finalized until sometime on Thursday. Reading the document, I found the answers to "What is the goal?" and "Why are we doing this?" I had the essential information I needed to get started. Now it was time to determine how I would pull off a training session in less than a week. My next step was to answer the questions that would help me formulate my plan. I went down the list: *What strengths are needed to reach the goal?*

I needed trainers who had strong remote training skills. I reached out to one of my peers who leads a team that handles national training sessions, explained the situation to him, and requested the use of four or five of his trainers. But I made it clear to him that I didn't need just anyone. I needed people who possessed the strengths necessary to conduct the training.

After laughing at the absurdity of my goal's timeline, he agreed to help and sent an email out to his team giving them advance notice that I would be reaching out. He advised them to look out for a meeting invite from me as early as an hour from then. His email simply included the answers to *what was needed* and *why*; the minimum to engage others into the initiative.

There wasn't much time and the trainers needed specific information very quickly, so they could prepare to train the staff. During the next hour, I completed a Training Needs Analysis which described the current state and what the expected outcome would be after the session (*information*). After the Needs Analysis, I completed a Lesson Plan. This included the purpose of the session, an introduction, the main points of the session, the materials and resources needed for each of the main points, and a closing statement.

It was time to practice what I preach.

I sent an invitation to all members of the National Training Team for an online meeting only ten minutes before the start time, with a note of "*Hope you can make it.*"

Only four people made it to the meeting. I started the call by providing them with more details about what the goal of the training was and explained why the company was making the change. I also affirmed that they possessed the strengths needed to carry out the task in such a short time frame.

To get their buy-in, I asked the trainers to volunteer for the roles they wanted. Two agreed to facilitate the sessions, and one agreed to assist the facilitator. The fourth was not going to be available during the session times, but he offered to record a session for distribution to those who couldn't attend one of the four live sessions we were planning. A fifth trainer reached out while we were in the meeting and offered to assist wherever needed but could not facilitate.

Within two hours of the original request, I had gathered information and created a plan. But, just like a road trip, I needed to continue to collect information so that I could monitor the plan.

Before the first training session, I met with the team of trainers to determine what their personal plans were for facilitating the sessions. I also explained that I would be attending each session and would provide feedback about what went well and, what, if anything, didn't go well (an After Action Review). During that call, as the project leader, I was also able to determine the possible outcome of the sessions.

Overall, the initiative was successful because we had the right information and a solid plan of action.

Just as the body needs water to stay alive, an initiative needs a great plan to be successful. After all, even if you have the right information, without a good plan, reaching the goal will be all but impossible.

Planning
Reflection Questions

Think about the challenge you identified on page 36 as you answer the following questions.

Individual Reflection

How will this goal be accomplished?

What strengths do I need to possess to carry out this initiative?

Do I fully understand the role I play in achieving the overall goal?

Leadership Reflection

Who has the strengths needed to carry out each aspect of this goal?

What is each possible outcome?

What is the most likely outcome based on the current factors?

When should benchmarks be set to ensure progress?

When there is marked progress or a setback, what was the cause?

Motivation

'I want to live.'

The Hike

Before we ever got our gear out of the car, I knew I needed to capture that great photograph. I knew it when we entered the enchanted forest. I knew it just beyond the tulip tree. I knew it when I took Kris's pack.

We were almost 90 percent there when I took her pack. Although I considered turning back myself, I also considered how I would feel about myself the next day. My mind fast-forwarded to the possible scenario twenty-four hours later:

My legs hurt like never before, the pain in my back, neck, shoulders, and legs was the most intense I've ever felt. I had a headache from dehydration due to the previous day's abandoned hike. I looked through the pictures in my camera and saw nothing more than a large tulip tree that represented a point three-quarters of the way into the hike, but not one photograph of Ramsey Cascade.

With that potential disappointment in mind, I continued for the next half a mile because I needed to finish what I started. I needed to feel there was purpose to the pain I felt. I needed to not give up.

Kris remembered what the falls looked like. She remembered what it felt like to finish the hike. She wanted me to see it. Ninety percent of the way through the hike, her motivation changed to a desire to not feel so much pain; she truly felt as though her body wouldn't make it to the waterfall.

The Real World

Motivation is what makes us begin something. It's also what pushes us to finish what we've started. Completely different things motivated Kris and me. I was even motivated by two completely different things in the first four miles. At first, I simply wanted to capture the photo, but as we neared the falls, my motivation was simply not to live with the regret of quitting before I'd gotten that photo.

We each started the journey the same way. We faced the same end goal, the same challenges, the same path, the same rocks to climb and roots to step over. When we continued after the first mile and a half, we had the same information and the same plan (to walk until we reached the waterfall). Everything we experienced was exactly the same. But the reasons each of us completed the hike were vastly different.

The reality is that we all do things for our own reasons. To put this concept to the test, imagine that a leader had accompanied Kris and me on that hike, and that leader wanted to "motivate us" to reach the waterfall. To keep me motivated, that leader might have encouraged and cajoled and reminded me repeatedly of how badly I wanted to see the waterfall. Throughout the hike, he might have tried to get me to imagine the exhilaration I would feel once I reached the end of the hike. Those images and reasons seem valid, but, for me, the pain I felt would have outweighed any desire for a feeling of accomplishment or for the reward of simply seeing the waterfall. Neither of those ploys would have been as strong as my own reasons for finishing the hike.

Likewise, had the leader tried to motivate Kris by telling her that this was the opportunity to capture the shot of a lifetime—the best photograph of Ramsey Cascade ever seen—or that she would regret giving up, she might not have continued. Neither of those reasons drove her to keep hiking.

Even though we were personally motivated by our own desires, had someone tried to push us continue for the wrong reasons, it's likely that we both might have turned around. Those reasons weren't bad, but they were wrong because they didn't matter to us. Ultimately, we would have determined that those reasons weren't worth the pain we felt. And with all the external motivation, we might have even forgotten about our own personal motivators—the real reasons we were on the hike in the first place.

Tapping into True Motivation

Trying to motivate others sounds risky, doesn't it? You may even wonder, if these are the risks of incorrectly assisting people in reaching their own state of motivation, why try? After all, if people are motivated to do things for their own reasons, and they have those reasons in mind, there's no point in reminding them why they're doing something, right? Wrong. Particularly in the professional world, people need motivation from a leader who understands them.

It's rare to find a front-line employee who wants nothing more out of his or her career than to make the company's leaders look good or to ensure the company reaches higher value on Wall Street.

During my seminars, I often start by asking the audience, "Why do you work?" It's always fun to hear the different responses. The list focuses on necessity. Some of the reasons that come up in every session include:

- To pay the bills.
- My kids need food.
- I need the money.

I then ask, "What do you *live* for?" This is where I begin to hear about people's hobbies and what truly excites them. This list comes from their character and their passions.

With their reasons for working and living identified on two separate lists, I then challenge the audience members to see if anything from the second list could be transferred to the first. The summary is that the first list represents surviving. The second is truly living.

My encouragement to the people in those audiences—and to you—is to remember that our careers should support our personal lives and not the other way around. Sure, I'm happy to receive a paycheck, but the real reasons I work include hiking, photography, and spending quality time with my wife and my family. To me, that's living.

The real question comes when an employee reflects on the value they receive from their employer (benefit - cost = value). The cost could be stress, time away from family, and getting up early, just to name a few. The list of benefits includes sense of purpose, vacation, recognition, health benefits, retirement, and, of course, rate of pay. Some of these benefits apply specifically to the workplace, but most cross over into our personal lives.

My challenge for you is this: Identify why you work. Keeping those reasons in the forefront of your mind will help you push through stressful, busy times, or, better yet, to find solutions that improve the value you perceive from your career.

Leading with the Right Motivations

If you are a leader, I have one more challenge for you: Figure out what the motivations for the people you lead are. In the business place, determine what each of your employees' professional motivators are. With your spouse and children, identify what they live for—what drives and excites them.

Leading with the right motivation can and should be applied to all endeavors—professional, volunteer work, and personal challenges.

My mom was recently hospitalized. After a week in ICU, five

surgeries, and the diagnosis of a terminal illness, she had no appetite and refused to eat. Already malnourished, there was no acceptable variance of eating less. She had to eat to stay alive.

The nurses and my family tried for days to convince her to eat. The nurses told us we could bring in her favorite foods. We did, and a few things got her excited, but after only a bite or two, she was done. One particular morning, I called to get a report from the nurse as I had every day for three weeks prior. The nurse told me that if Mom didn't start eating, she would have to have a feeding tube. When I got to the hospital that morning, I was the only visitor. Her breakfast had just been delivered. I pulled up a chair and stated that I needed to ask her a question that required a completely honest answer regardless of how she thought I would feel about her answer. She looked concerned and asked, "What is it?"

I held her hand, looked into her eyes and asked, "Do you want to live or are you ready to give up?" I had been there with and for her through each challenge, and she knew she could be honest with me, and that I would continue to sit by her side no matter what her answer was. Still, I wanted her to know she could be honest with me so I spoke softly, "Either way is okay and if you want to give up, you certainly have that right."

I wanted to know what she really wanted—what she would be willing to live for—before suggesting that she eat more. My next words were entirely dependent on her response. If she was ready to give up, I would work with the nurses to determine how to make her comfortable, otherwise, I needed to tell her the consequence of not eating. I was her medical representative, so I already knew that she didn't want to be put on any type of life support.

She squinted her eyes at me and very quickly said, "I want to live. Why are you asking me that?" I told her that if she didn't start eating, she would need a feeding tube for nutrition and explained to her that it was a form of life support. I knew that not being on life support was a motivation for my Mom. She told me she wanted to live—and to do that, she would have to eat. That very simple plan would allow her to reach her goal.

She immediately started eating the eggs and asked me why no one told her it was that severe. I explained to her that we had tried for weeks to get her to eat and it wasn't that severe until this morning. The news did not make her want to eat or magically bring her appetite back after being under anesthesia five times, but it did give her enough information to do what she needed to do (even though she didn't feel like doing it) to live without life support. I helped her reach her own state of motivation.

Motivation drives our actions—even in dire or uncomfortable circumstances. After all, Kris and I had no information and no plan, but we hiked for nearly eight and a half hours and ascended 2,100 feet up a mountain while dehydrated, weak, and in severe pain before walking back down another 2,100 feet on a fast-food breakfast. Just imagine what you can do with good information, a solid plan, and the right motivation!

Motivation
Reflection Questions

Think about the challenge you identified on page 36 as you answer the following questions.

Individual Reflection

Am I doing this for my own reasons or somebody else's reasons?

What's in this for me if I carry out this challenge?

What will it mean to me if I succeed?

What will it mean to me if I don't succeed?

Does somebody else know my answers to the above questions?

A few things for a leader to consider:

- No one is carrying out this challenge solely because they want me to succeed.

- I will lose great people if they are not personally motivated.

- I cannot motivate other people. I can only help them realize their own motivation.

Leadership Reflection

Answer all the above questions as well as the following:

Do I know what motivates the others involved in this goal?

Have I used their motivators respectfully to help achieve results?

9

Support

'Four more, man.'

The Hike

We were still in the first two miles of the hike when I started looking back over my shoulder regularly to check on Kris. By the final half mile, I noticed she was checking on me, too—a clear indication that I was showing similar signs of dehydration. We always check on each other when we hike, but this time was different. Neither of us asked "How are you doing?" or "How do you feel?" Instead, we regarded each other from head to toe, looking into each other's eyes to make sure we were focused and watching for shaking arms and legs. From the lack of sweat rolling off our flushed faces, it was obvious that we weren't doing well. Regularly checking on each other confirmed the rapid decline of our condition.

Throughout the hike, we supported each other in a variety of ways. Kris understood my motivation and believed in my talent as a photographer. Although she felt exhausted and wanted to turn back, she insisted I continue so I could capture the photograph I'd imagined so many times along the way. At that final water crossing, the moral support she offered meant as much—perhaps even more—than the direction she gave. Likewise, by recognizing her misery and carrying her backpack, my support meant she was physically able to continue. And, as terrible as we both felt on the return trip, we offered support to the barefoot family. We had no new information to offer each other or anyone else. Neither of us had the strength to physically support the other on the way back. Motivation was no longer a factor because we *needed* to get back to the car even more than we *wanted* to. For the rest of the hike, the support we offered each other subsisted of nothing more than encouragement and an understanding of how the other felt. We supported each other's' mutual goal of getting back to the car.

The way we crossed the first bridge might seem like a perfect example of support, but in reality, it's a better example of course correction after recognizing that a team member needs support.

Think back. We were experiencing the same hike. I made the occasional obligatory check on Kris, but upon reaching the bridge, I walked straight across it and was going to continue on. I left my partner behind, without considering she might need more support from me to successfully navigate this new obstacle. The crossing wasn't lower for me than it was for her. It didn't shrink as I crossed it. We were faced with the exact same challenge. But, what was easy for me terrified my partner.

The Real World

Here's my point: While it was never my intention to leave Kris behind, neglect to consider her viewpoint, or be a thoughtless partner, that's exactly what I did at that water crossing.

The reality is most of us forget to consider that others may need support to tackle a challenge we've aced. It's not that we are unwilling to provide additional support. Often, like at the water crossing, we simply don't recognize that support is needed, and as a result, people get left behind and the end goal suffers.

Leaders may not view the new obstacle as anything other than a bridge to cross. The fact that their neglect is simply an oversight offers little consolation to those left behind. In fact, their lack of support may be seen as a blatant disrespect or purposeful neglect and cause followers to feel isolated or undervalued.

Leaders don't hold the sole responsibility for providing support. Every member of a group, whether it's a business, a volunteer organization, or a family, is responsible for recognizing and offering support to team mates. Personally, the highest level of support I've experienced was in the Army.

The saying, "There's one in every group," was true of our platoon in basic training. We had a soldier who joined at the maximum age of thirty-four. He struggled to keep up with the rest of us, who were still in our late teens and early twenties. He struggled with everything, especially physical training (PT). He couldn't do as many push-ups or run as far and as fast as the rest of us. In most environments, a person who can't keep up is shunned and written off with a dismissive complaint, "He shouldn't be here." But not in our platoon.

Fifty of us were taking the final PT test required for graduation. The test consisted of two minutes of push-ups, two minutes of sit-ups, and a timed two-mile run. He was the last one to start the test. Our entire platoon was there to support him; there was nowhere we would have rather been than right there cheering for him. The minimum requirements reduced by age group. To pass, he had to complete twenty-five push-ups. He was solid until he got to about seventeen. At first, a few low voices called out, "Come on, man, you can do this." As he continued, the voices gained volume and passion until forty-nine of us were screaming our support, "FOUR MORE, MAN! COME ON! THREE MORE! YOU CAN DO IT! DUDE, YOU GOT THIS!"

His arms shook uncontrollably. "Pause at the top, man, and knock out two more." He stopped at the end of his twenty-third push-up, took a couple of deep breaths, and let out an incredible warrior yell as he dropped his body weight down for push-up number twenty-four.

We were clapping and yelling all around him. As fluid as a river flowing over rocks, he dropped again and lifted himself up for the twenty-fifth time. Just as the strength in his arms gave out, he turned his head so the right side of his face landed on the ground. We pulled him up and continued to celebrate his victory. Every one of us had already passed our tests, but we were committed to the spirit of "No man left behind." He completed the sit-ups and two-mile run requirements surrounded by the support of his platoon.

Support does not have to be as loud and obnoxious as we were that day. Recently, I took a leave of absence to take care of my parents. During that time, one of my co-workers reached out at least weekly to ask how I was and if there's anything he could do to help. He never mentioned business; he just offered me support throughout a difficult time.

During that time, Mom was getting ready to go into her fifth surgery. My three siblings and I gathered from around the country in the pre-op area and realized it was the first time in twenty-four years we were all in the same room together. We needed one another's support as much as our Mom needed ours.

The challenges we face in the business world may not always be life threatening, but when you understand that everyone experiences the challenge together, it's easy to see the need for every individual to come together and support both the goal and one another. It can be as simple as checking on one another regularly and openly discussing personal feelings about the change, as well as its impact on business success. Having the opportunity to voice concerns or questions—and to feel as if those thoughts are valued and respected—helps prevent that detrimental feeling of isolation. Be available to your team, be it family or business, and encourage each member to support not just the mission but their teammates as well. Mutual support empowers you to get through life's challenges without burning out.

Support
Reflection Questions

Think about the challenge you identified on page 36 as you answer the following questions.

Individual Reflection

How do I feel about the challenge?

Have I shared my feelings about the challenge with others?

Do others support the work I'm doing?

When there is a setback, can I turn to my team for support?

Am I willing to support anyone on my team, without reservation, when needed—including success and setbacks?

Leadership Reflection

Do I promote team support and leadership support?

Would all members of my team support each other in successes and setbacks without reservation?

Do all of my recent actions with my team reflect my support of them?

Leadership

'We trusted each other explicitly and without reservation.'

The Hike

On our hike, neither Kris nor I were "in charge" of making sure the hike was successful. This day, just like every other day, Kris and I were peers. She had information that I didn't have and vice versa. Early in the day, she led the way. After all, she had been to the waterfall before. I acted as the leader when I proposed going to the enchanted forest and offered two separate options to determine our course. After the first mile and a half, the leadership role shifted again when she gave further information and put the decision in my hands by asking, "What's it going to be?"

As we continued, we both acted as leaders by checking on each other. At the bridge, I led as I crossed while suppressing my own fear of heights then taught her to do the same.

I took the lead by carrying her backpack and she demonstrated leadership when she limited our time at the waterfall to fifteen minutes.

We were peers and equals who accepted the fact that during different parts of our challenge, one or the other was better equipped to lead. We were open to each other's guidance, direction, and support. We trusted each other explicitly and without reservation. As a result, and in spite of being ill-prepared for the journey, we survived the challenge and accomplished our goal.

The Real World

The Boy Scouts of America was my first memorable experience within a structured-leadership organization. As a scout, I had a patrol leader, a senior patrol leader, several assistant scoutmasters, and the scoutmaster. As I started my rank progression, the senior patrol leader periodically came over and asked me about what I was learning. After listening to my responses, he would give me a tip that wasn't in the handbook. I felt as though I was getting super-secret information about first aid, knot tying, and wilderness survival! That encouragement made me feel better about myself and my achievements.

I used many of the skills I'd learned from the senior patrol leader, especially on camp outs. Time after time, I approached him for confirmation or to ask him to clarify things I didn't understand. More clearly than his words, I remember that, after responding to my inquiry, he would firmly squeeze my shoulder, smile big, and send me on my way with a strong pat on the back.

One day, the scoutmaster asked me what I thought about the senior patrol leader (SPL) and the way he treated me. I replied that he was great and really helpful. The scoutmaster seemed puzzled and said he had rarely seen me with the SPL. In fact, the SPL was concerned because I never went to him for help.

Confused, I told him about all the times that I'd gone to the SPL for help. We both had an *aha!* moment when we realized that the person I was referring to was not the SPL; he actually held no official position in the troop. I looked at the scoutmaster and replied very seriously, "Well, he should be."

During the next few months, the scoutmaster worked with the real SPL to improve his leadership presence within the troop. I continued to go to the other scout for assistance and worked on becoming someone other scouts could come to for help. It wasn't lost on me that leaders don't always hold titles and those with titles aren't always leaders. That meant I could be a leader—even without an official title. The peer I regularly went to for help did end up getting promoted to patrol leader and the real senior patrol leader developed his leadership presence and became a trusted resource for many of us.

The Second Question

My co-workers and I were recently invited to share our workplace insights with a manager who was relatively new to the company. During our one-on-one meeting, the manger asked if there was anything I wanted to share. I trusted this person and shared a few of my concerns. Shockingly, the manager pounded the desk and blurted out, "Why does everyone keep telling me the same thing? I didn't get this position for being an idiot!" In that instant, I learned that this person was more interested in managing than leading. I thanked the manger and escorted myself out of the office.

Not a day goes by that this "leader's" underlings aren't reminded of who's in charge. That attitude is the reason I immediately applied for another position. I'm not interested in being *managed* nor are most of the people who work for you. Management is important for success, but here's what you must remember: Businesses are managed; people are led.

When people ask me about the difference between a manager (or other leadership title) and a true leader, I ask two questions. The first is, "Who do you receive direction from?" The second is, "Who makes you truly want to come to work every day?"

The answer to the first question is generally a person with a title. The answer to the second question—Who makes you truly want to come to work every day?—is the real leader. If you're lucky, the person with the title and the person who inspires you are the same. But many times, a leader doesn't hold a title. Although we often think of people with titles as leaders, the truth is, having a title is not leadership. Managing or supervising are not the same as leading, nor does providing direction equate to leadership.

Management, supervision, and providing direction are more closely related to administrative tasks than they are to leadership. In contrast, leadership is a character trait, which is why the greatest strategy an organization can implement is to promote proven leaders into titled positions.

Identifying Leadership Qualities

So, how do you identify leadership qualities in others? How can you make sure you choose leaders to help drive the mission of your organization? Begin by identifying "Who?" and "Why?"

Who do others go to

- For information?
- To hear a plan?
- For a voice of reason to help them through the day?
- When they need support?

These are the leaders of your organization.

The next question you must answer is "Why are others choosing those individuals as their leaders?"

It's human nature to self-select leaders who provide information, motivation, or support. Such leaders can provide a grassroots support system for growth. But if you, as a leader, don't properly prepare and equip your leaders, misinformation and misdirection can become a huge problem. Consider how the following scenario might play out in your organization. (For the purposes of this illustration, the term "manager" indicates a person in a position of authority.)

The organization you are a member of has experienced many changes in the past few months. The manager is happy to see people interacting throughout the day, but he also recognizes that morale is dropping.

He decides to have one-on-one conversations with the organization's team members. The manager asks each person to describe the changes he or she has recently experienced or been affected by and to identify the purpose for each of those changes.

As the conversations proceed, some groups seem to have accurate information and a realistic purpose, while others are responding with information and purposes that are not part of your organization's initiatives. This information is not only wrong but also quite negative. The manager respectfully asks where the information came from, only to discover that the source is two tenured people. It becomes clear that people are going to these two individuals to get information, to hear a plan and a voice of reason, and to ask for support.

Clearly, these two individuals possess leadership qualities that appeal to others. The challenge for the manager in this scenario is to engage these employees in a way that enhances their existing leadership characteristics and use those characteristics to wield more positive results throughout the organization.

One way to do this is to determine where the people with good information got it, and then pair several of these people with positive leadership traits with those who have been inadvertently leading others astray with inaccurate information. Additionally, you may even choose to include these lay-leaders in meetings or correspondence to ensure they spread the right information. If possible, empower them with communication responsibilities so they can update others with the accurate information. When people with positive leadership characteristics are given positional roles, they can accomplish great things.

Commit to Others' Success

When I applied for my current position, it was new to the company and reported directly to the regional manager. I had worked briefly with that manager and was genuinely excited to have the opportunity to work directly for him.

During the interview process, the regional manager left the company to pursue outside opportunities. I felt like I was a passenger on a rudderless ship. I reflected extensively on the fact that if I were offered the position, I would be working for an unknown manager I might not like. I considered pulling my name out of the running but decided to take the risk and continue the process.

Interview after interview, I asked for details about this new position. Every response came back the same: the details would be determined when the new regional manager was selected. A few months after I got the position, the new regional manager was named. In my fifteen years with the company, I had never met her. I discovered that she had years of sales and management experience but no experience in operations.

The first time I met with her, she asked me, "What excites you?"

I rambled for twenty minutes about hiking in the Smokies, photography, and Kris. She told me my excitement was infectious, and that my stories made her feel as if she'd hiked through the Smokies even though she'd never been there.

During the same conversation, she told me that, initially, she would learn more from me than I would from her, but she was committed to shifting that in the shortest amount of time possible. It took her less than six months to learn enough to make tough decisions without engaging anyone else in the process, and she achieved outstanding results.

Her entire focus was making me a better leader and manager. She provided support by recognizing a job well done and never missed an opportunity to hand out credit, rather than taking it for herself. I always felt like I knew what was happening in the company, and why, because she made me feel like we were equally responsible for the success of the organization. With every company initiative she shared with me, she asked what part my team would play in the overall plan. I remained committed to her success because she was committed to mine. In her first year of regional management, our region went from the worst in the company to the best.

Without her accurate information, planning, support, and taking a genuine interest in my motivators, as well as those of all of my peers in the region, we would have never reached that status.

We met every company and regional initiative as a result of her leadership, while all the tough decisions she made were part of her management responsibilities.

I felt like we were peers. We were equals that accepted the fact that during different parts of our challenge, one of us was better equipped than the other. I led her and she led me. We were open to the guidance, direction, and support from the other. We trusted each other explicitly and without reservation. That commitment served us and our organization well.

Leadership
Reflection Questions

Think about the challenge you identified on page 36 as you answer the following questions.

Individual Reflection

From whom do I get my information, support, and motivation regarding plans for the future?

Is the information, support, and motivation enough to carry out the plans of the organization?

Does anyone turn to me for answers?

Do I portray positive leadership characteristics when others turn to me?

Leadership Reflection

Do I engage all leaders of the organization, titled and untitled, in planning and dissemination of information?

If people are going to others for information, support, and motivation regarding plans for this initiative, what are they getting from those individuals that they are not getting from me?

Do I treat the titled leaders who report to me as if they are equally responsible for the success of the organization?

Do I have a vested interest in knowing what excites the members of this organization?

The Giving and Receiving of Water

Dehydration is one of the most unpleasant things I've ever experienced. During my stint in the Army, my unit spent one August at the National Training Center in Fort Irwin, near Barstow, California, which is roughly fifteen miles off the southern tip of Death Valley. I'll summarize the experience.

Death Valley. In August. The end.

One morning, one of the platoon sergeants made everyone gather around for some good news. He was so excited that we could feel it. We knew what was coming before he ever said a word. We were certain that, even though we were supposed to spend the entire month there, he was going to tell us that we were going home although it had only been two weeks. We were so certain that many of us (including me) almost didn't go to this impromptu gathering of soldiers. But we went, and when we had all arrived, he made his big announcement. He was standing in the hatch of the armored personnel carrier with a huge grin on his face, looked out at the crowd of sweat-drenched soldiers and shouted, "It's only going to get up to 126 degrees today; we'll get some relief from the heat!" Then after an evil laugh, he said, "That's all. Goodbye," and ducked out of sight.

We spent the full month there.

In Death Valley, we each drank six to ten canteens of water—more than two gallons—every day. We arrived at Fort Bliss in El Paso, Texas, on a Saturday just before Labor Day, and all we wanted to do was to drink anything that had flavor in it, anything but water. Saturday night was a great relief from the desert of California. It was wonderful to be clean, wear shorts, and drink sugary drinks with so much flavor. I reveled in the variety of tastes through Sunday night as well, until the strangest feeling came over me. We were out enjoying the local music scene when I began to feel tired and weak. I asked a friend to take me back to the barracks and most of the group headed back with us. My buddies piled into the back of my friend's pick-up truck, but I rode in the cab with him and his wife. During the eight-mile drive back to the barracks, he asked several times how I felt, and I kept telling him that I was tired but all right. I could hear people asking what was wrong with me, why was I slumped over, but my friend assured them I was just tired.

When he stopped to drop us off at the barracks, I heard his wife say, "I'm a little worried. This isn't normal. He has all of his weight on me, but I don't think he's sleeping."

My friend pulled me upright but momentum kept me swaying in his direction until all of my weight was on him. He pushed me upright again, but I fell over on his wife's shoulder and then into her lap. The strange part was that I wasn't sleeping or unconscious; I knew what was going on around me, but I couldn't speak or move. I couldn't even hold myself up. He yelled for me to wake up, and although I heard him just fine, I couldn't respond.

Extremely concerned, he patted me on the arm and told me not to worry; he was taking me to the Army hospital. His wife switched places with me, so I could lean on the door. Fully conscious, but unmoving, I watched the world fly by as my friend raced to the hospital.

The truck screeched to a stop in front of the emergency entrance, and my friend ran inside to get help. Two people with a gurney hurried out and opened the passenger door, catching me just inches before I hit the ground. I tried to respond when they asked me my name, but nothing came out. They lifted me on the gurney and rushed me through the double doors.

The next thing I remember is that it was light outside and a guy in a white coat was asking how I felt. I realized I could speak and move— my body felt almost normal. "What happened?" I asked.

While checking my vitals, he explained that I'd been dehydrated. "You need to thank your friend for bringing you here when he did," he said. His next words puzzled me. "You had about an hour left."

"An hour left for what?"

Looking me straight in the eye, he said, "To live."

I thought I'd had plenty to drink in the past couple days, and I hadn't been sweating nearly as much as I had in the desert, but during my time in Death Valley, my body had gotten used to taking in two gallons of water every day. It takes a while for the body to adjust to changes in hydration, but I had stopped drinking water completely. All the sugary drinks I'd been consuming didn't provide the hydration my body needed. In fact, without the three bags of saline I received at the hospital, I would have died that night.

The Secret to Success

Of course, that was an extreme case of dehydration. By comparison, the dehydration Kris and I experienced on the hike was minor. But even mild dehydration decreases our ability to think and perform well.

Metaphorical water—information, planning, motivation, support, and leadership—exists in every initiative we create or are a part of. But sometimes that water doesn't reach everyone. Even if it's available, some people may be mildly dehydrated—others may be dying of thirst.

Here's the big secret to success: We must all recognize the specific water we need and ask for it. If we see that others don't have enough water, we need to share what we have.

Recognizing the Need for Water in Others

In a team environment, whether it's professional, volunteer work, a family, or among friends, water levels must be continually monitored.

Team members who don't have enough water will show signs of disengagement, lack of concern or care, and little or no initiative. Normally talkative people become quiet. They may isolate themselves by not joining in during team events, stating they have too much to do and don't have time to step away from their responsibilities. They may come in late or call in sick more frequently than normal. I call this professional dehydration.

When this dehydration occurs, the first thing to determine is which of the five waters of success are lacking. Too often, instead of doing a proper analysis, leaders tend to jump right into performance management and hold the employee 100 percent accountable for their lackluster results. A better course of action is for leaders to first hold themselves accountable for not providing the right amount of water.

As peers, we have a tendency to identify these thirsty individuals and, whether consciously or subconsciously, shun them; removing the support they desperately need. Rather than shut off their supply line, we should increase our support. You can do this by simply acknowledging their needs. That doesn't mean you should approach a co-worker or teammate and say, "Your engagement seems low. Tell me how you're feeling." But you can offer support by simply asking, "You don't seem like yourself lately. Is everything all right?" The person's initial response might be, "Yeah, everything's fine," when it's obvious that's not the case. That's ok. Opening a line of communication allows them to come back sometime to discuss what's on their mind.

Recognizing the Need for Water in Ourselves

It's also important to be able to recognize when you are professionally dehydrated. When you feel stressed, worried, or disengaged, pause for a moment and consider each water of success and determine which one you may need more of. Ask yourself these questions:

- Do I have all the information that I need?
- Do I know what the plan is?
- Do my motivators truly drive me to succeed?
- Do I feel supported by the people I need support from?
- Are my leaders going in a direction that I am willing to follow?

Once you identify what's lacking, it is your responsibility to yourself and your organization to ask for that specific type of water. And if you're still thirsty, ask for more.

Water All Around Us

When we finished our hike, Kris and I still had half of the water we started with, yet we were dehydrated. We had plenty of water for the journey; we just didn't drink enough of it. The truth is, if we had drunk all the water, we still might not have felt great; we weren't in the best physical shape, remember? Still, we would have felt much better and our packs would have been a good deal lighter.

When you're facing a challenge and feel "dehydrated" emotionally or mentally, remember that there is water all around you. You might be lacking some of the "waters" you need to succeed, but I can almost guarantee that what you need is available to you—you just have to find the right person and ask for it. Somebody has the information you need. Somebody has a plan or can help you create your own. Somebody can help you reach a state of motivation. Somebody is willing to offer support. Somebody can lead you to success.

When you need water, ask for it. When you have some to spare, offer it. When water is within reach, don't conserve it, drink it. Never stop asking, *How much water do we have?*

The Return to Ramsey Cascade

It was four years after our initial hike to Ramsey Cascade and Kris and I were nearing the end of our twelve-day vacation in the Smoky Mountains. Sitting on the balcony of our cabin, we reflected on the previous ten days.

The first full day of our vacation, we first hiked to Cummins Falls, a three-mile, round trip hike through a gorge along the Blackburn Fork of the Roaring River. We left Cummins Falls State Park and, around 2:00 p.m., we hiked the half-mile round trip to Lost Creek Falls, southeast of Sparta. Since we still had some daylight left, we ventured over to Rock Island State Park to see Great Falls, Twin Falls, and a number of unnamed waterfalls which seemed to appear from nowhere out of the rocks.

The second day of our vacation began at Burgess Falls State Park, where we hiked three miles to see three separate waterfalls including the featured Burgess Falls. Later in the day, we drove to see Ozone Falls—no hiking, just beautiful scenery.

By the end of the third day, we had hiked a combined twelve miles or so and had seen fourteen waterfalls. We spent seven more days hiking a combined fourteen miles in several locations in the Smokies. Day by day, we'd built up our endurance, which allowed our bodies to prepare for the longer hikes, and we didn't lose a single day to the agony of sore feet.

Two days before the end of our vacation, we sat on our balcony overlooking the mountains and talked about what we'd seen and done during the past week and a half. When I asked Kris what she wanted to do the next day, she looked at me with a hint of a smile and said, "I don't know. How much water do we have?"

I laughed out loud and the discussion began.

"We know what to expect this time. And we've already hiked more than twenty miles."

The motivation behind her desire for enduring the Ramsey Cascade hike? "I want to beat that big mountain," she told me.

My motivation? I wanted to hike the eight miles without feeling awful at the end of the day. I was happy with the photo that I captured four years ago but believed I could do even better.

I knew my motivation was strong enough to help me overcome the obstacles of hiking to Ramsey Cascades again. I asked Kris if she felt that her motivation was strong enough to get her to the waterfall. With a nod, she confirmed it was.

We planned carefully, gathering supplies and deciding what time to wake in the morning. We also determined exactly what each of us would carry: Kris would take the hip pack filled with two water bottles, a first aid kit, and protein bars. I would carry the water-filled backpack with a lightweight tripod strapped to it, as well as two spare water bottles and my camera case.

The alarm sounded at 6:00 a.m., and after showers and a healthy breakfast, we gathered our things, loaded the car, and drove towards the Greenbrier area of the Great Smoky Mountains National Park. We talked excitedly until I parked the car; then we both fell silent. Neither one of us spoke as we got out and looked at the sign at the trailhead with the words: RAMSEY CASCADE.

Our silence wasn't an indication that we were reconsidering our decision to return to the waterfall. Instead, it was a moment taken to humbly compose ourselves. Without saying a word, we looked at the woods and thought about the trek ahead.

With a shared sigh, we broke the quiet moment and readied for the hike, strapping the gear to our backs and waists and changing our footgear.

It was time. We glanced at each other and started across the foot-bridge. We talked quite a bit as we walked along the logging road, stopping now and then for photographs. We were almost shocked when we reached the point where the old road ended and saw the sign, RAMSEY CASCADE 2.5, with a beautiful display of rhododendron beyond it. We couldn't believe we had made it there so quickly—and without taking a break! With smiles on our faces, we entered the enchanted forest, hiking single file.

We stopped periodically to drink water as we continued up the mountain. Every once in a while, we met others on the trail—some passed us quickly, others stopped to take their own pictures. A couple of early hikers, already on their way back down the mountain, greeted us and said, "We've been coming here for twenty years and have never seen the water so strong coming off the falls." Their enthusiasm invigorated us. We felt like children anticipating Christmas morning!

We were still going strong when we reached the bridge that spanned over the raging river beneath. Recent rains caused the current to flow much faster than it had four years earlier. One slip would have been detrimental. But Kris, though she felt fearful, was determined with each step. She made it across in less time than before. Before continuing up the mountain, she turned around and cussed the bridge with pride.

Shortly after crossing the bridge, we found a nice spot to rest. Sitting on some large rocks bordering the water, we took off our packs, drank water, ate a protein bar, and took in the amazing scenery. Four years prior, we'd been so focused on our pain that we'd barely noticed the beauty of this stretch of the journey. This time, we felt as if we were seeing the forest with new eyes. Reminiscing, I asked Kris when she had first wanted to turn back on our previous trip. She told me she had wanted to quit long before the water crossing. But on this day, aside from the normal burn that comes with hiking, her legs felt great.

We took a few pictures at the tulip tree and crossed several small streams created by the recent rain fall. And this time, we navigated the steepest parts of the hike by stepping on rock after rock without the need to stop and catch our breath. Around the three-mile mark, we started taking more frequent breaks to both rest and drink water, but none lasted longer than three minutes. As before, we knew the falls weren't far when the air cooled and silence overtook the woods. A few steps farther and we could hear the sound of rushing water in the distance.

We climbed confidently between the huge boulders and kept going. The small water crossing that had confused me last time was now a swollen creek. On the other side, beyond the trees, we saw a huge wall of water—Ramsey Cascade. What a beautiful sight it was that day! The mist raced off the waterfall and enveloped us as we stood on the huge rock—the same one on which we had taken photos of ourselves last time.

I climbed around the rocks and in the water to angle for an even better photograph. Even being fifty yards downstream from the base of the falls, the mist covered my camera lens within seconds. Standing in the cold mountain water, I snapped photographs for at least a half of an hour.

We stayed almost an hour before starting back down. The muddy trails were slippery, something we noticed more on the hike downhill. We went back through the narrow pass between the boulders, past the tulip trees, and by the time we made it back to the logging road, our legs felt the painful strain of all the muddy miles we'd hiked that day. Stopping at the trailhead footbridge, we took several photographs upstream before heading back to the car. Thirty minutes later, we loaded our gear in the car, put on fresh, dry socks (Thanks, scoutmaster!), and returned to our cabin.

Our decision to return to and conquer the Ramsey Cascade hike freed us from the demons of doubt and discouragement that we had picked up four years prior. Perhaps not coincidently, the second hike took place on July 4th. I'm thankful, though for the incredible challenge of our first attempt because it taught us about the necessity of the waters of success—information, planning, motivation, support, and leadership. With these waters, you too can overcome any challenge.

How much water do you have?

**Scan the code to view a photo album
of the Ramsey Cascade Trail.**

Also from

DAVE BURGESS
Consulting, Inc.

Teach Like a PIRATE: *Increase Student Engagement, Boost Your Creativity, and Transform Your Life as an Educator*
By Dave Burgess (@BurgessDave)

Teach Like a PIRATE is the *New York Times'* best-selling book that has sparked a worldwide educational revolution. Translated into multiple languages, its message resonates with educators who want to transform school into a life-changing experience for students.

The Innovator's Mindset: *Empower Learning, Unleash Talent, and Lead a Culture of Creativity*
By George Couros (@gcouros)

In *The Innovator's Mindset*, George Couros encourages teachers and administrators to empower their learners to wonder, to explore—and to become forward-thinking leaders.

Pure Genius: *Building a Culture of Innovation and Taking 20% Time to the Next Level*
By Don Wettrick (@DonWettrick)

In *Pure Genius*, Don Wettrick inspires and equips educators with a systematic blueprint for teaching innovation in any school.

Master the Media: *How Teaching Media Literacy Can Save Our Plugged-in World*
By Julie Smith (@julnilsmith)

Written to help teachers and parents educate the next generation, *Master the Media* explains the history, purpose, and messages behind the media.

P is for PIRATE: *Inspirational ABC's for Educators*
By Dave and Shelley Burgess (@Burgess_Shelley)

In *P is for Pirate*, husband and wife team, Dave and Shelley Burgess, tap into years of personal experience and draw on the insights of more than seventy educators to offer a wealth of ideas for making learning and teaching more fulfilling than ever before.

Learn Like a PIRATE: *Empower Your Students to Collaborate, Lead, and Succeed*
By Paul Solarz (@PaulSolarz)

In *Learn Like a PIRATE*, Paul Solarz explains how to design a supportive, student-led classroom where improvement, rather than grades, is the focus.

Ditch That Textbook: *Free Your Teaching and Revolutionize Your Classroom*
By Matt Miller (@jmattmiller)

Ditch That Textbook is a support system, toolbox, and manifesto to help educators free their teaching and revolutionize their classrooms.

50 Things You Can Do with Google Classroom
By Alice Keeler and Libbi Miller (@alicekeeler, @MillerLibbi)

Complete with screenshots, *50 Things You Can Do with Google Classroom* provides ideas and step-by-step instructions to help teachers make the most of Google Apps for Education (GAfE).

The Zen Teacher: *Creating Focus, Simplicity, and Tranquility in the Classroom*
By Dan Tricarico (@thezenteacher)

In *The Zen Teacher*, educator, blogger, and speaker Dan Tricarico provides practical, easy-to-use techniques to help teachers be their best—unrushed and fully focused—so they can maximize their performance and improve their quality of life.

***EXPLORE* Like a Pirate:** *Gamification and Game-Inspired Course Design to Engage, Enrich, and Elevate Your Learners*
By Michael Matera (@MrMatera)

Michael Matera reveals the possibilities and power of game-based learning in EXPLORE *Like a Pirate*. Readers learn how gamification strategies can enhance (rather than replace) existing curriculum be applied to any grade level or subject.

Your School Rocks... So Tell People! *Passionately Pitch and Promote the Positives Happening on Your Campus*
By Ryan McLane and Eric Lowe (@McLane_Ryan, @EricLowe21)

School principals Ryan McLane and Eric Lowe want to help you get the word out about the great things going on in schools today. *Your School Rocks... So Tell People!* is practical guide that helps teachers and administrators stay connected with their communities.

Play Like a Pirate: *Engage Students with Toys, Games, and Comics to Make Your Classroom Fun Again!*
By Quinn Rollins (@jedikermit)

School can be simultaneously fun and educational. In fact, as Quinn Rollins explains in *Play Like a Pirate*, when class is engaging, students are more likely to remember what they learned.

Acknowledgments

From Pete

To my wife and best friend, thank you for challenging me to always be my best. During that quiet ride home from Tennessee in July 2011, you encouraged me to find lesson and tell the story about that hike we took to Ramsey Cascade a week and half before. You have always been my biggest fan.

From Kris

Mom and Dad, you showed me the right way to live and I will forever be grateful.

Thanks to Art and Cathy for your encouragement and pride in our accomplishments and our potential.

Thanks to Marti Sholty for being a role model and never giving me an ounce of slack when it comes to being my very best.

Mostly, thank you, Pete, for getting me up the mountain that day, but more than anything, for always being my rock and a constant source of encouragement, even in the darkest of days.

From Both of Us

We both want to recognize the support of our families. You have always believed in us. For our friends who offered to read an advanced copy and provided us with comments and a first edit, specifically Andrea Muncie, Bobby Seng, Colleen Honeyman, Lesley Fields, Penny Flippen, and Shannon Peffer: Thank you.

Thanks, also to Kellie Palacios, Kris Hardy, John Bonetsky, Susan Walls, Joy Eppig, and Marti Sholty for contributions to the Introduction.

Thank you, Gray Flores, for providing us the lead of our publisher.

Thank you, Dave and Shelley Burgess, for taking a break from the pirate life to talk to these literary nobodies.

Thank you to the editors, Erin Casey and Jenna Lang. Because of you, buyers will read the entire book instead of closing it after the first paragraph. You made us sound really good.

Thank you to Genesis Kohler for the cover design. I wouldn't blame you if you retired after having to work with us on all of our requested changes.

To Mom, the scoutmaster, the drill sergeant, the good and bad leaders, the boss, the peer, the SPL, the people returning from the waterfall (even though you have no concept of distance), the authors of the book on how to finish furniture, the weatherman sergeant, and, of course, Mark Jordan, who saved Pete's life: None of this would be possible without you.

Thanks to the mountains of Tennessee and North Carolina for saving us from ourselves.

Finally, to Pete's Dad: We got the cow out of the ditch.

About the Authors

Pete Nunweiler is an Army veteran who served as a canon crew member in the Third Armored Cavalry Regiment in El Paso, Texas, from 1992–1994. He served as a citizen soldier in the Indiana National Guard through 2002 as a nuclear, biological, and chemical warfare non-commissioned officer.

Since 1998, Pete has worked as a field training manager, providing knowledge to front-line service providers for a large payroll organization. He has been recognized as one of the top service providers in the company.

Pete is an Eagle Scout from Troop 18 in the North Star District of the Crossroads of America Council of the Boy Scouts of America and continues to contribute to the Boy Scouts.

Kris Nunweiler manages the Indianapolis branch for a large payroll organization. In twenty-one years of leadership, Kris has never lost an employee reporting directly to her for voluntary or involuntary termination. She considers this one of her greatest accomplishments.

Pete and Kris married in June 2009 and currently live in Indianapolis, Indiana. They travel to Tennessee and North Carolina regularly to entertain a passion for photography that began during their honeymoon. You can view their portfolio and purchase their photographs including "Ramsey Cascade" and "Ramsey Cascade Trailhead" at NunweilerPhoto.com.

CPSIA information can be obtained
at www.ICGtesting.com
Printed in the USA
BVHW03s1443260418
514392BV00024B/1037/P